John Williams

The World's Witness to Jesus Christ

The Power of Christianity in Developing Modern Civilization

John Williams

The World's Witness to Jesus Christ
The Power of Christianity in Developing Modern Civilization

ISBN/EAN: 9783337033545

Printed in Europe, USA, Canada, Australia, Japan

Cover: Foto ©Lupo / pixelio.de

More available books at **www.hansebooks.com**

THE BEDELL LECTURE FOR 1881

THE WORLD'S WITNESS

TO

JESUS CHRIST

The Power of Christianity in developing Modern Civilization

BY

THE RT. REV. JOHN WILLIAMS, D.D

Bishop of Connecticut

NEW YORK
G. P. PUTNAM'S SONS
27 AND 29 WEST 23D STREET
1882.

COPYRIGHT BY
G. P. PUTNAM'S SONS
1882

Press of
G. P. Putnam's Sons
New York

EXTRACTS

From the communication of the donors to the Board of Trustees of the Theological Seminary of the Diocese of Ohio and Kenyon College.

CLEVELAND, June 21, 1880.

GENTLEMEN:

We have consecrated and set apart for the service of God the sum of $5,000, to be devoted to the establishment of a lecture or lectures in the Institutions at Gambier on the Evidences of Natural and Revealed Religion; or the Relations of Science and Religion.

We ask permission of the Trustees to establish the lecture immediately, with the following provisions:

The lecture or lectures shall be delivered biennially on Founders' Day (if such a day shall be established), or other appropriate time. During our lifetime, or the lifetime of either of us, the nomination of the lectureship shall rest with us.

The interest for two years on the fund, less the sum necessary to pay for the publication, shall be paid to the Lecturer.

The Lecturer shall also have one half of the net profits of the publication during the first two years after the date of publication. All other profits shall be the property of the Board, and shall be added to the capital of the lectureship.

We express our preference that the lecture or lectures shall be delivered in the Church of the Holy Spirit, if such building be in existence; and shall be delivered in the presence of all the members of the Institutions under the authority of the Board.

We ask that the day on which the lecture or the first of each series of lectures shall be delivered, shall be declared a holiday.

We wish that the nomination to this lectureship shall be restricted by no other consideration than the ability of the appointee to discharge the duty to the highest glory of God in the completest presentation of the subject. We desire that the lectures shall be published in uniform shape, and that a copy of each shall be placed in the libraries of Bexley Hall, Kenyon College and of the Philomethesian and the Nu Pi Kappa Society. Asking the favorable consideration of the Board of Trustees,
  We remain with great respect,
        G. T. BEDELL,
        JULIA BEDELL.

The Board accepted the gift, approved the terms, named All Saints' Day, November the first, as Founders' Day, and made it a holiday.

LECTURE I.

I COUNT it no small privilege to be permitted to join in the services of a day like this. The foundation on which I am honored with the position of first lecturer, and which has been so nobly provided for all coming time by the pious forecast and thoughtfulness of those whose good works for "Christ and the Church" have been so manifold, is itself something to which a day of grateful commemoration might well be devoted. It takes its place, however, with other commemorations which carry us back over the history of three generations. I cannot forget, this day, that he who came hither long years ago, to lay the foundations on which this goodly superstructure has arisen, came from the diocese in which my lot is cast; and I, therefore, rejoice the more that I am permitted to share in the services of the first celebration of Founders' Day.

On such a day, too—how appropriately joined

to the commemoration of All Saints—it cannot, I think, be inappropriate to speak of the evidences of Christianity. Since whatever other evidences there may be found—and God be praised for their manifold variety—the grandest of all must ever be the lives and deaths of that "great cloud of witnesses of whom the world was not worthy."

But I must not linger on thoughts like these, grateful as they are, and I turn to address myself to my proper duty.

When we speak of Christian Evidences what a boundless field of thought and discussion opens before us! We touch the world of nature and the world of man. We come into contact with natural science, with human history, with the inductions of observation, with the deductions of reason, with weighing of testimony, with the profoundest needs and the loftiest aspirations of humanity. We have to deal with the internal, or subjective, evidence in the individual mind, and with those proofs that are addressed to the reasoning faculties in man.[1]

Moreover, when from such general survey as we can make of this field of thought, to

---

[1] Palmer's *Doctrine of Development and Conscience*, p. 2.

which there seem to be no limits, we descend to details, how endlessly various we find those details to be. To say nothing of Apostolic days, from the time when Justin Martyr[2] began the first Apology for Christianity " by urging the claims of truth," down to the present day, each succeeding age has brought out its own special line of attack, demanding a parallel line of defence or assertion. The general character of the conflict has been marked by a changelessness that is even sublime, but the successive forms of the onset and the resistance have shifted like the rapid movements of some vast battle-field.

Out of all this has arisen the necessity of guarding against two great mistakes: first, that of forgetting in our attention to details wider and more comprehensive lines of argument; and secondly,—if indeed this is not a form of the mistake just mentioned,—that of giving to some immediate and pressing attack an importance which does not fairly belong to it. For instance, so much attention has been given of late to scientific difficulties,[3] to the relations, as

---

[2] *First Apology*, Sec. 2.

[3] Perhaps one might better say the difficulties raised by writers on science. Ernest Naville well says: "There have often been

the phrase goes, between science and religion, that we have left much out of sight the great historical argument. Nor only that; where the historical argument has been worked, it has sometimes been with an attention to details— the value and power of which should by no means be underrated—that has led men away from those wider and grander views which that argument can employ, with such persuasive power, in asserting the claims of the Faith and the Church of Jesus Christ our Lord.

In the two lectures which it has become my duty to deliver, I propose, by God's blessing, to present one form of the general historical argument which seems to me to be a strong one; and that not so much in the negative way of defence, as in the positive way of assertion. I am not at all sure that the charge will not be brought against positions and method alike, that they are quite old-fashioned and out of date. I am altogether sure that they ought neither to be forgotten nor abandoned.

Let us find, then, our starting-point in a fact which no man will question. When we look

---

conflicts between theology and science, or rather between *theologians* and *naturalists;* for between belief in God and science there is a profound harmony."—*Le Christ*, p. 53.

LECTURE I.

around the civilized world we find everywhere in it some form of Christianity.

And whatever the form may be, it rests for its authentication and its motive power, nay, for its life and being, on one person, Jesus of Nazareth.

Whatever else these forms may differ in, they all agree in this. They all assert that at a certain definite period in the world's history, there lived in Palestine one who was known as Jesus of Nazareth, and that he was the author of that Faith and the founder of that Church which are embraced in the general term Christianity.

From this unquestioned and unquestionable position we advance to another equally undoubted and unassailable. We find, on testimony which can neither be gainsayed nor evaded, that at the time and in the place asserted, such a person as Jesus of Nazareth did actually live, and that from Him Christianity came as from a founder.

It was the fashion in some quarters, in the last century, to assert that no such person as Jesus Christ ever existed;[4] but such a position would hardly be assumed to-day. Indeed it

---

[4] Dupuis, for instance, in his *Origine de tous les cultes*, published in 1795.

could not be without shaking down all historic testimony whatever, and reducing all the history of all time to a dream or a falsehood.

The scornful words of Tacitus,[5] "The author of this name [Christian] was Christ who, in the reign of Tiberius, was punished with death by the Procurator Pontius Pilate," are the testimony of a heathen to a person whose existence is as truly historical as that of the Emperor of Rome or his representative in Palestine. Nor is this testimony confirmed merely by the utterances of believers of the early days and by the historic creeds of all the Christian ages. The early opposers and maligners of Christianity, be they Jews or Pagans, be they represented by their own words, or in the apologies of those who replied to them; the early heretics and corrupters of the Faith, be they Ebionites or Gnostics; all these unanimously attest the historical verity of the existence at a given time in Palestine, of a person known as Jesus of Nazareth. All equally bear witness to the fact that Christianity came from Him. To deny this is simply to destroy all history.

To these unquestionable facts let us add a

---

[5] *Annals*, Lib. XV. c. 44.

third, namely, that at the time when He whom we call our Lord was to be born, men were everywhere yearning and hoping for a better day than the world had seen; a day of deliverance from manifold miseries internal and external, a veritable golden age, wherein the world that seemed dying around them, should receive a fresh life—even a new creation.

The fire-worshippers of Persia, the Chinese disciples of Confucius, looked for the regeneration to arise in the West. The nations of the West, on the other hand, looked eastward.[6] Tacitus speaks of the general persuasion, founded on priestly writings, that in those days the East should grow powerful, and those who should come from Judea should be masters of the world,[7] and Suetonius[8] repeats his words; while the vision of the new and glorious age is sung by Virgil[9] in words which, seeming to echo those of the Evangelic Prophet, are themselves echoed in many a mediæval Christian hymn.

Standing, now, at that period in human history where we find Jesus of Nazareth living

---

[6] Schaff's *Apostolic Church*, p. 184.
[7] *Hist.* Lib. V. c. 13. [8] *De XII. Cæsar*, Lib. VIII. 4.
[9] *Eclogue* IV.

upon earth, and where we are breathing this atmosphere of expectation and listening to these words of hope, let us look back over what was then the long past of the story of our race and see, at least, something of the work done and the preparation made for a new order of the ages, as we say to-day, a new departure for humanity. Just how this review falls into my proposed line of argument will appear as we advance.

At first thought such an undertaking, even when preceded by and accompanied with the declaration that only the most general and even cursory review will be attempted, must appear almost absurd.

The field, it will be said, whether in reference to time or place, is so vast, the details are so manifold, that to attempt to cover the one and present the other in a single lecture can only be an act of folly. There is, however, a consideration which must very greatly modify this obvious criticism.

Frederick Schlegel long ago declared that the number of really historical countries, when these are compared with all the countries of the world, is relatively small.[10]

---

[10] *Phil. of History*, p. 108, Bohn's Ed.

As the stream of historic life and progress has flowed onward from its source in Central Asia, it has moved within narrow limits, and its course has been ever westward. Confining our view to the eastern hemisphere, and we need not now look beyond it, we find this stream of historic life mainly limited, even to our own days, by the twenty-fourth and sixtieth degrees of north latitude. Those limits embrace not more than fifteen really historical countries, and even of these not all had fairly entered on their development "when Jesus was born in Bethlehem of Judea." Indeed if we fix our eyes on the middle country of Western Asia, as it lies on the two great streams of Tigris and Euphrates, and between the Persian and Arabian gulfs and the Caspian and Mediterranean seas, and then look on to Arabia, Egypt, Asia Minor, Northern Africa, Greece, and Italy, we shall have glanced at all the countries which, to the time of our Lord, had entered into that development of the race which really constitutes universal history.

For universal history, it must be remembered, is not a mere collection of the detailed histories of single nations. It concerns itself with the general destiny of mankind, and does not allow this main subject to be lost in the multitude and variety of details. As, amid the millions of men who are born and live and die, there are few who can be called historical men, so it is also with nations. Of these there are, and there must be, many which "serve only as a mark or evidence of some particular stage of civilization, without of themselves holding any particular place in the general history of our species, or conducing to the social progress of mankind, or possessing any weight or importance in the scale of humanity." I know, indeed, and would recognize the sublime truth with awe and thankfulness, that to the all-seeing eye of God every human soul has its own great history reaching beyond the grandest destinies of time into the mightier destinies of eternity. But this is God's view, not ours. When we deal with human history we are limited as He is not. We deal then with humanity, its triumphs and its failures, its gains and its losses, its advances and its retrogressions, as a whole. Mankind is, and must be "all mass to the human eye, even though it is all individual to the Divine."[11]

The task, therefore, which I have proposed

---

[11] Mozley's *Univ. Sermons*, p. 121.

LECTURE I.

is not so hopeless as at first thought it might appear. Difficult as it may be, it is not altogether an impossibility.

Far back, then, in the story of the human race, so far back that, in the mist which shrouds them all visible forms are dim and phantom like and all thoughts of men come to us in fashions that are vague and ill-defined, I seem to recognize a yearning for wider unions and more extended brotherhoods than those of family, or tribe, or clan, or even nation. What is it, this mysterious impulse that carries men's thoughts and wishes onward? It looks marvellously like an instinct implanted in man's nature; an instinct which shall one day find the thing that fits it and satisfies its longings, albeit, in the mean season, it may go far astray in its search and waste its strength on ways and methods that end in nothing. No doubt this instinct was early seized and perverted by that "spirit of enterprise and ambition" which sprung up in and emanated from the "great middle country of Western Asia, the native seat and cradle of conquest." It was seized and perverted so early that men hardly remember how true and genuine the instinct that lay behind the perversion was. And yet its influence was incalculable. It entered largely as a living force into that successive uprising of empires which the visions of the prophet Daniel so marvellously foreshadow, and which gather to themselves so much of the older history of the human race.

Cast your eyes along that great "course of empire;" the Babylonio-Assyrian, which first of all brought men together in imperial union; the Medo-Persian, which bore, at last, the Orient to the shores of Europe; the Græco-Macedonian, with its rapid rush of conquest, which carried Europe back into the East, and in its break-up did such marvellous work for the future of the race; and the Roman, which in its irresistible march swept the wide world. Was all this, think you, merely the outcome of the ambition of one or another strong and masterful man? That marched, doubtless, at the front, but it was able to march there, and to march to conquest, because of the deep instinctive feeling of mankind, that their highest achievements and their grandest destiny required a union and an organism wider and deeper than any that family or tribe or nation could present to them.

This instinct, too, it was that from time to time spoke out in words of sage or poet weary of evil and yearning for good. It shaped the re-

LECTURE I.

public of Plato, so noble amid all its impracticable ideals and abstractions. It animated the cry of Terence, "I am a man and nothing human is alien to me." It spoke in the verse of Claudian, when he sung of Roman citizens—all one nation—who drank from the Rhone and the Orontes, and whom Rome, in an empire that should know no end, cherished as a mother rather than ruled as a mistress.[12]

So had this course of empire run, carrying along with it men's instinctive hopes and longings, and such were its outcomes when our Lord was born. It held in its bosom—so far as they shared in the world's true history—the human race. And more than that, whether there was in the world only a desolation that went by the name of peace, or whether the peace was real, there was such peace that the symbolic temple of Janus was closed, and some men may have dreamed that in this Universal State, the strong desire of man for a universal brotherhood of humanity had been attained.

Was it so? Had the new order of things, the golden age, really arrived? Were the longings of all the ages met? A thought of which,

---

[12] *De Laudibus Stiliconis*, Lib. III., line 150 ff.

purposely, I have not yet spoken, answers those questions, and answers them in the negative. Only two factors in the building up of empires have been named: one the enterprises of ambition, the other the longing for human brotherhood. There was another, which gave the first its greatest power and crushed down or swallowed up the second, and that is found in the debased passions and ferocious hatreds of men.

Till these were touched no empire met the longing desires of men, or could satisfy the instinct of which I have been speaking. The great disturbing cause, the root of bitterness, remained. Wherefore the apparent peace and repose of that year of Augustus in which wars, for the time, had ceased could not, in the very nature of things, be a finality. Human needs were not met nor were human longings satisfied. Another and a higher peace must descend, and " be made visible on the earth—and along with that higher and diviner peace, a new and spiritual combat, waged not with the warlike parties of old, nor even with external and earthly power, but with the secret and internal cause of all the agitations and all the injustice in the world." [13] How, by whom, in what, this peace

---

[13] Schlegel, *ut sup*. p. 203.

LECTURE I.

and combat were to come, I shall try, in due time, to show. Just now we must pass on from these very general views to others that are more specific.

Were I, now, to take the countries and peoples we are to consider in strict order of chronology, Egypt would claim our first attention. But its great preparatory work for a crisis in the world's history and a new order of mankind really took place in the break-up of the Græco-Macedonian Empire; and, therefore, I turn from it to that noblest land of the ancient world —Greece.

Nature herself marked this land as one of manifold activities and varied life. Think of " its advantages in reference to navigation, commerce," and colonization. It is situated in the immediate vicinity of the three great quarters of the globe, and is washed on three sides by the sea. Look at its remarkable coast line, so irregular, so indented with bays and harbors, and so enormous in proportion to the superficial area of the country.[14] A nation dwelling in such a land must do what the dwellers in the vast plain of Central Asia never could have

---
[14] Heeren, *Man. of Ancient History*, p. 90. Freeman's *Historical Geography*, Introd. § 2.

done; they must build ships, they must engage in commerce and maritime adventure. They are very likely to become a colonizing people. They may, if they will, carry, as England and America have done in our time, their language into every part of the known world.

Then take into view the varied surface, mountains, valleys, plains, which this country presents; the variety of climate which is thus produced; a variety, however, which does not interfere with its general mildness, and which, taken in connection with its numerous small streams and the qualities of its soil, make up a country in which "every branch of cultivation may be prosecuted equally and in conjunction."

Consider, finally, the manifold diversities in race—composed of so many heterogeneous elements,—in civilization, in history, in legislation, in forms of government, in habits of thought and life, in poetry, arts, science, in a word in all that goes to the make up of a nation's being, which this wonderful land presents; contrast all this with "the seclusion and monotonous character of Asiatic influence, the generally unchangeable uniformity of Oriental society," and you have the pledge of an intellectual development and an artistic culture, the promise of a bloom and a glory that you find nowhere else in all the ancient world.

The pledge and the promise were fulfilled. As near as human effort can approach perfection without supernatural aid, so near to perfection Greek culture came. All that painting and sculpture can achieve without the inspiration of a divine ideal to fill the artist's soul and guide his pencil or his chisel, that Greek art achieved. All that philosophy can accomplish without a divine law to shape its precepts, and a divine sanction and a divine life to give it a motive power and make it effectual to the advancement of mankind, that Greek philosophy accomplished: while Greek commerce and colonization carried throughout the world—making it a universal medium of communication—a language richer and more harmonious, more capable of giving to words nice shades of meaning, and expressing all subtle play of thought, and distinguishing in utterance things that differ, than any language that human lips had ever spoken. As one looks upon it all, its brightness dazzles and confuses,

" . . . . sinking far,
And self withdrawn into a wondrous depth,
Far sinking into splendor without end."

Alas that it was all so powerless! Alas that it left Greece "a lazar house of morals." [15]

Naturally, I might turn here to Judaism and the Jewish Nation, and speak of what they directly did for and contributed to the universal history of the world. For reasons, however, that need hardly be stated in detail, I wish, in the present argument, to keep outside the limits of revelation, and, therefore, will only say of Judaism that with all its great endowments, its knowledge of the one true God, its pure morality, its covenant privileges, it had lost its living power, and was ending in those three miserable "tendencies which are usually found to arise when a religion decays, namely, sanctimonious formalism, trifling infidelity, and mystic superstition." [16]

Still, there was an indirect work of Judaism which does come very directly into our present line of argument. It is found in the contact of Judaism with Heathenism; and its story—briefly to be told—opens out some of the most striking pages in the history of the world.

Judaism had, indeed, touched heathenism from its early days. Necessary contacts with

---

[15] Sewell's *Christian Morals*, p. 43.
[16] Schaff's *Apostolic Church*, p. 172.

surrounding tribes and, later on, the widely extended commerce of Solomon effected this.

The Babylonish captivity must have greatly multiplied these points of contact, and given permanence and power to the influence which they enabled Jewish faith and thought to exercise. But there is one place to which, above all others, we must look for the nearest approach that Judaism made, whether to Greek or Oriental thought and culture, and for the greatest influence it had upon or received from them.

It was a dream of Alexander the Great to build, on the coast of Egypt, a city that should bear his name and be a centre of commercial enterprise as well as the metropolis of his western empire. His dream was more than realized. For under the first three Ptolemies, whose reigns filled out the years of a century, Alexandria became a centre not less of science and learning than of trade. The days of these Ptolemies were days of desolation and destruction in the world. But for these great princes, so far as man can see, science and learning must have perished from the earth amid a darkness that might be felt. But under their fostering care science and learning "found more than a shelter, they found a rallying point." Nor did the glory and the power of Alexandria pass quite away till an illiterate barbarian sacrificed its magnificent library in the brutal ignorance of his execrable fanaticism. A thoughtful scholar of our own time has said, speaking of Christian Alexandria, "to the last, Alexandria fulfilled its mission, and we still owe much to the spirit of its great teachers, which, in still later ages, struggled, not without success, against the sterner systems of the West." [17]

Jews, Greeks, Egyptians, were the chief classes of the inhabitants of this most attractive city; but mingled with them were the representatives of almost every nation of the then known world. And thus it came to pass that all varieties of mind, all forms of thought, were brought together there. Greek activity, vivacity and restless energy; Oriental conservatism, faith and quietism; Jewish shrewdness and love of speculation; creeds of East and West; clashings and strifes of dogma; indirect influences of various literatures and philosophies upon each other; all these brought together in Alexandria, and then carried out from it, must have told mightily on the mind of the world. It is often and truly said—sometimes (and then untruly) in a carping

---

[17] Prof. Westcott in *Smith's Bible Dict.*, art., "Alexandria."

way—that "the literary school of Alexandria was critical and not creative." Still let us not forget that there language was studied, the records of all the past collected, and the exact sciences perfected. Well does Heeren ask, " Suppose the critic's art, which now grew up, could not form a Homer or a Sophocles, should *we*, had it not been for the Alexandrians, be able to read either Homer or Sophocles ?" Above all, let us remember that there the elder Scriptures were translated into the then universal language of mankind, and, in the venerable Septuagint version, given to the world. And here, for the present, I leave this centre of thought and influence, only adding that we shall have occasion to recur to it again.

Over all the lands at which we have glanced, over all the wrecks of all the great ancient empires, over Greece and Palestine and Egypt, swept the resistless power of Rome. Ordained to rule the world, the Roman Empire completed the work that Alexander had begun. It broke down many a barrier, it bridged over many a gulf, and, to speak of no other things which it accomplished, it brought the whole civilized world into one *State* and ruled it by one *Law*.

As Greece had brought men together by her

ships which navigated that great central sea around which were gathered all the elements of human civilization, so Rome, by her marvellous far-stretching roads, bound together all parts of her world-wide empire. These wonderful constructions, "issuing from the Forum of Rome, traversed Italy, pervaded the provinces, and were terminated only by the frontiers." They ran "like railroads, straight as arrows," from one extremity of the empire to the other.[18]

Never before had the human race been so brought together, never, apparently, so put in the way of being welded into one state, as by these two agencies—the law and the roads of Rome. And yet no real welding was accomplished. There was outside pressure enough and to spare. The difficulty was internal, and though it was the resultant, doubtless, of many factors, there was one thing above all others, I think, which produced it. It is difficult to state this fact in a brief way, and yet the attempt must be made.

Law, then, presents itself first as strict and

---

[18] Gibbon, Vol. I, p. 31, Harper's Ed. Stanley's *Eastern Church*, p. 182, Am. Ed. Gibbon says that from the wall of Antoninus to Rome, and thence to Jerusalem, the road measured four thousand and eighty Roman miles.

absolute; and secondly, as tempered and moderated by considerations of equity. Now "if this last conciliating principle does not pronounce its sentence, or if it is not attended to, extreme injustice only can spring from this rigid and inflexible application of extreme law." Then the more law there is the less justice will there be. *Summa lex summa injuria*, is the proverb in which this truth has been expressed. As one has well said, "Woe to mankind, woe to every individual, woe to the world, were they doomed to be judged according to this rigid justice, and only by it, even by HIM, who alone has the right and the power to dispense such rigid and severe justice unto men." Only one who is incapable of error can dare to judge in this wise. And He—His holy name be praised!—does not so judge men. He takes all circumstances, all conditions, all opportunities, all degrees of *light* and *knowledge* into account, and not only "in the midst of judgment remembers mercy," but tempers all strict law by a most righteous equity.

Now Roman law had in it little or no room for equity. It was strict, absolute, inexorable in the letter. When Roman jurists said, *Fiat justitia ruat cœlum*—let justice be done though the heavens shall fall—they meant just that strict, absolute, inexorable letter. So that, however true and good that letter might be, its administration, untempered by the manifold circumstances of which equity takes account, could be neither good nor true. It must provoke reactions, oppositions, contests. If it did bind men externally in iron bonds, it yet drove them asunder by internal repulsions. It did not, it could not, meet men's needs. Its defect was fundamental, nay, it was fatal.

This was bad enough. But there was more and worse. This false theory of absolute law led on to political idolatry of the state. For that which administered such a law, might well seem the impersonation of that great deity of the *Prometheus Vinctus*, whose two demons, Force and Might, presided over the nailing of the victim to the rock; nay, the impersonation even of that all-powerful Necessity which is over all, and to which Homer makes Zeus himself an obedient slave.

In time this deified state became incarnate in the persons of successive emperors, and then the emperor was also deified, and Nero and Caligula were gods! No possibility of worship remained to heathen Rome " but the worship of power," and this power was incarnate in the sovereign of the world. It had all ended in this. The gods of the old mythology had vanished away before the "unknown God" was preached at Athens by St. Paul.[19]

Let me now gather up and summarize these manifold preparations for a possible future of humanity, a new order and a nobler one, which, in our rapid survey, we have noted. I have not even tried to speak of all these preparations. Only the more salient and important have been named; while, for the reason already mentioned, the direct preparations of the Jewish Œconomy have been purposely passed by, and its indirect work alone has been considered.

The point in human history at which we stand, it must be remembered, is just before our Lord was born. As we look back over the wide field we have glanced at, what do we behold?

We see that deeply rooted instinct of humanity which longs for even universal brotherhoods and unions, living and working through the ages, and, even when it is not actively at work, living still in yearning souls. We see the arts,

---

[19] Schlegel, *ut sup.* pp. 264-267. Conybeare and Howson, *Life of St. Paul*, c. xxvi.

philosophy, laws of reasoning, outcomes of imagination, carried to a point beyond which human powers can scarcely go. We see a universal language, so perfect that the highest praise that can be given to any later tongue is that it approaches its marvellous capabilities. We see Greek ships carrying men from one region to another; and Roman roads completing the opportunities of intercourse thus given to the world, breaking up old isolations, breaking down old barriers, so that "many shall run to and fro, and knowledge shall be increased."[20] We see scholars gathered at Alexandria just when the "abomination of desolation" seemed to be sweeping over the world, and then scattered from thence over the world again, with the sacred books of the Jew translated into the universal language. And finally we see the iron Roman law, the law of "the ever prosperous, the eternally powerful, the world devouring, the people destroying Rome," binding the nations into one by its strong external bonds, even though powerless to prevent internal disunions and repulsions.

What a spectacle it is! What solemn

---

[20] Dan. XII., 4.

thoughts of its own present does it awaken! What possibilities for a future not its own does it suggest! Are all these things to come to nought? Are they simply to flash upon the sight as meteors flash across the sky and then go out in darkness? Is there to come, for the world, no person, no system, no institution that can gather up all those agencies with all their possibilities and powers, and use them for an advancement of the race such as has never before been reached? The world has, as we may say, stopped for a space in its troubled career. There is, outwardly at least, the hush of peace among the nations. And in that hush these questions come to us. How the men of that age pondered them; what the men of that age felt of hope and anticipation or of fear and despair; what the story of the then long future has to say in answer to them, will, God willing, engage our thoughts when we meet again.

Meanwhile, it is well to remember that when men, in various lands and in successive ages, have been laboring without concert, each doing his own work and then lying down in death; and when each of those isolated works is still found to have its place and function in some grander nobler work, which takes them all up and uses them for its own great purposes; more than that, when men's perverse and evil passions are, in their outcomes, made themselves to serve such higher purposes and help on such more beneficient and gracious ends, he cannot be a weak man, or the victim of a foolish superstition, who shall say, "The Lord is King, be the people never so impatient; He sitteth between the cherubim be the earth never so unquiet."

LECTURE II.

The close of my previous lecture left us not amid the ruins, but amid the possibilities, that surrounded the men of the period when Jesus of Nazareth was born in Judea. It can scarcely be necessary to recapitulate those elements of a possible advance, those factors in a possible future for humanity. In all of them, under the guidance of God, men had "builded better than they knew." Their rough hewing had been shaped for higher ends than they could dream of. At this point, we turn from the past to glance briefly at the then present before we look at the coming future.

And first, we ask, How did the men of the time regard these various elements, factors, possibilities? What thoughts were awakened, what energies were aroused, what impulses were given by them?

The view which these questions open to us is a strange one. Were we dealing with anything but human nature and its workings, we might well turn away in despair from its inconsistencies and contradictions.

Nothing is more striking, as we look back upon the times we are reviewing, than the profound and utter hopelessness for the present that everywhere we see and hear. Poets, historians, naturalists, moralists are all at one in this. Everywhere there is this undertone—not always an undertone—of blank despair. It sounds forth from song and satire; sometimes bidding men to snatch the passing pleasure of the day, its wild revelry and wanton mirth; sometimes urging them to seek for refuge in a proud, self-sufficient, heartless resignation— that was no real resignation—the principles of which, if carried out, must logically end, as they often actually ended, in suicide. Thus men were vibrating between a frivolous Epicureanism and a self-deified Stoicism.[21] It was under the

---

[21] Both these philosophies were really philosophies of despair. The one made happiness, the other virtue the supreme good. But the happiness of the Epicurean was a serenity too superficial and frivolous to be disturbed in its round of pleasure ; the virtue of the Stoic was a passionlessness too proud and self-contained to care for anything. Neither system had that in it which could meet men's wants. See Bp. Lightfoot's "St. Paul and Seneca," in his *Commentary on the Philippians.*

dominion of this dark despair that Rome's great historian began his history with words so fearful, speaking of nothing upon earth but "darkness and cruel habitations," beholding nothing in the heavens but manifest tokens of coming vengeance. I need not swell the catalogue with names. There is all around the same cry of woe; man's wretchedness, death's blessedness are its burden.[22]

But along with all these cries of despair over the present, there were also utterances of hope for the future. I have already spoken of these, and need not repeat what has been said before. How the deliverance was to come, who was to be the deliverer, no man could tell. Easterns were looking westward, westerns were looking eastward, each away from themselves to other and far-off regions, each forward from the hopeless present to some unknown future. It is a strange spectacle. The longer we dwell on it the stranger it appears. Let it suffice to have thus brought it, in its contradictions of despair and hope, before your minds.

---

[22] It is obvious to refer to Horace, Juvenal, and Persius. The passage specially referred to in Tacitus is, *Hist.* Lib. I. 3. See also for a summary, not at all exaggerated, Dr. Schaff's *Apostolic Church*, pp. 158–59.

We see to-day that there was nothing, at that period, in all the world that could lift man out of the mire and clay, and set his feet upon a rock, and so order his goings that he might walk in light, and live and move under the power of what should be, in very deed, a new creation. And, besides, that which was to the men of that time the impenetrable darkness of a hidden future, is to us the clear and distinct history of all the centuries of a lengthened past; and to that history we look—we have a right to look—for the answer to these cries of despair, these murmurings of hope, that reach us across the vast expanse of ages.

There were religions and philosophies in the world then, others have made their appearance since. What one of these, if any, has taken up those various elements that we beheld, and used them all for the advancement of the race? What one of these has proved itself possessed of the capability of universal adaptation, of a permanence which is living and not fossilized, and of the power of continuous and limitless expansion?[23] These three marks or signs I hold to be not only noteworthy but crucial. A

---

[23] Eaton's *Bampton Lectures* for 1872. Lect. I.

system in which they are not found—whether it contains doctrinal or ethical truth or both—cannot be one fitted to meet the hopes or fulfil the destinies of man. It may contain elements of truth, and those elements may give it—must give it—a certain degree of power. They may adapt it, within circumscribed limits, to the attainments of a race, an age, or a country. They may give it a permanence which turns out, on examination, to be the permanence of a sealed up corpse that crumbles into dust when light and air are let in upon it. They may work for it an expansion that may continue for a time, but that comes at last to an end. Such a system carries within itself its own doom of death. It proves itself incapable of doing that for humanity which the very instincts of humanity demand. There is still another question that may well be asked, although it may appear to be covered by those that have gone before. What system has most thoroughly developed human intelligence and given the greatest impulse to the arts and industries that in our time have achieved such triumphs? I hold that any system, institution, religion[24] which, in the lapse

---

[24] I use this word, fully holding Christianity to be more than *a*

of ages, has shown itself competent for such achievements as these questions indicate ; which has been able to gather up all those preparations of all previous time and use them for the best interests of the race ; which has shown itself possessed of capabilities of adaptation to all nations under all conditions of life, raising them, meantime, towards, if not to, its own ideal of what men should be ; which has proved itself permanent, not as being fossilized into immobility but possessed of an ever animating life ; which has exhibited a power of expansion that, though sometimes checked, has never been destroyed, and to whose advances no limits can be set ; which has most thoroughly developed human intelligence and given the largest impulse to these arts and industries that contribute to the noblest civilization ; I hold that such a system, institution, or religion has vindicated its right to hold the world as its heritage, and the nations as its possession. More than that, I claim for it the right to demand that in the absence of any other adequate explanation of its origin, its nature, and its powers, its own account shall be accepted. Nor is more

---

religion, which man might contrive: even *the religion* which God revealed. But the word is accurate enough for my purpose.

included in this demand than a truly scientific method must necessarily require. Canons of historical criticism can no more rightly be *a priori*, arbitrary and antecedent to the facts of history, than canons of good writing can properly be *a priori*, arbitrary and antecedent to good models in composition. All true canons of criticism, whether historical or literary, are —as Pope[25] said long ago of the latter—"discovered not devised." In either case facts precede theories. Theories, indeed, must come out from facts and not be imported into them.

Taking, then, the testimony of almost nineteen centuries, what answer do we obtain to the questions, gathered up into one, that we have been asking? Where do we find the system, religion, institution, which has met the conditions presented to us, and accomplished, with whatever drawbacks, the work for the race for which all previous history had been the unconscious preparation?

I anticipate your answer to this question as you anticipate mine. In truth there is but one answer that can be given. It is the system of Christianity, the religion of Jesus Christ, the

---

[25] *Essay on Criticism.*

institution known as the Christian Church, that has accomplished this; not Confucius, not Buddha with the Sutras, not Mohammed with the Koran, not anything that has been, or that is in the world has accomplished this, except Jesus Christ and His Church. Of Christianity only can that be said which Montesquieu has said of it,[26] "The religion of heaven has not established itself by the same methods as the religions of this world. Read over the history of the Church and you will see the prodigies of the Christian religion. Has it resolved to enter a country? It knows how to open the gates of that country, and can use all instruments that present themselves. Sometimes God employs a few fishermen, sometimes an emperor on his throne. Does the Christian religion conceal itself in subterranean hiding-places? Wait a moment and you will hear the imperial majesty speaking in its behalf. It crosses seas, rivers, mountains; there are, in truth, no obstacles that can arrest its march. Are human minds repugnant to it? It overcomes that repugnance. Are customs, usages, edicts, laws opposed to it? It will triumph over natural conditions, over

---

[26] *Defence de l'Esprit des Lois;* article Tolerance; vol. iv. p. 274, ed. 1772.

laws and legislators." Strange and striking words these! but how strictly true! What a picture they present of the march of Christianity along the historic pathway of the world, taking up as it advances all the factors that the ages have prepared for a possible future, and from them and with them enabling men—by its spirit, in its power, through its life—to work out all that is best and noblest in that civilization of whose triumphs, on every side and in all directions, we are never weary of making our boast.

Look at Paul the Apostle of the Gentiles, as, under his appeal to Cæsar, he comes to the imperial centre of the world. Mighty in the Hebrew Scriptures, trained in Jewish learning, not untrained, assuredly, in Greek letters, speaking the universal language—Greek, crossing the Mediterranean in a Greek ship of Alexandria, advancing, after he reaches the shores of Italy, towards the capital on a Roman road, coming to be tried at a Roman tribunal, and by forms of the world-wide Roman law, what a living prophecy, so to speak, he is of the progress of the Faith and the Church of Jesus Christ. Except the mighty events of our Lord's own life, to which there can be no parallel nor approach,

I know no sublimer spectacle in the history of the world than is exhibited by the apostle standing, if not literally still very really, in the presence of the Emperor of Rome. Both are representative men as well as individuals. Each represents a system—and the systems so represented are alternative possibilities for the historic world. The one centres in the Roman Emperor, the other centres in Jesus Christ; and one or the other is to mould the world. Which of them shall it be? That represented by the emperor who witnesses to, and in some sense records, the failures of the past; or that represented by the apostle who is the living prophecy of the possibilities of the future? History has answered that question, and we all know what the answer is.

To attempt to follow out this answer in all its multitudinous details, multiplying themselves through eighteen centuries, would be a simple impossibility. It would involve a review of philosophy, science, art, literature, the great industries of civilization, and many other things which could be adequately exhibited only in volumes upon volumes. The result, however, of such a survey may be expressed in the briefest of brief statements. All these things have been most fully and thoroughly developed in Christian countries and under the influences of Christianity.

If there are any things on which our present civilization specially values itself, these are its great attainments in science and in the industrial arts. We hear and speak of these attainments continually ; and assuredly they deserve to be heard about and spoken of. How are we to explain the fact that they are exclusively the possession of Christian countries—so exclusively, that other countries have them to-day only as Christian civilization has introduced them, and sometimes (as in the case of China) introduced them in the face of violent opposition ?

The fact is admitted by those who have no wish to admit it, no prejudice, as we say, in favor of Christianity. Indeed, it is too patent to be denied. In 1877, at a reunion of naturalists at Cologne, a Berlin *savant* and professor said : "Paradoxical as the utterance may seem, modern science owes its origin to Christianity." In the report of the French commission on the Exposition of 1851, we find a manufacturer saying, "The exposition has proved to all the world that industry really exists only in Christian countries."[27] He means, of course, the great industries, those that deal with the wonders of mechanism and the use of natural agents.

What does this fact mean, and what is meant by citing it? Is it meant that Christianity has directly concerned itself with that knowledge of nature, its laws and forces, which constitutes science, or with the application of that knowledge which results in the great industries of our time? Assuredly not; to assert that would be both false and foolish. No! but that the intellectual movement which Christianity rouses up in men, just how we need not ask, has taken on, and then given out, the impulse which has wrought these wonders. The writer from whom I have cited the testimonies just given, has placed this matter in so clear a light that I avail myself, with a single change, of his striking words. They occur at the close of a brilliant lecture on "Christ the Teacher." "If on going out of this hall you should say to a friend whom you chanced to meet, 'We have just learned that Jesus Christ invented machines, telegraphs, and railways,' you would provoke a smile. But if you said, 'We have had pointed

---

[27] Cited by Naville, *Le Christ*, pp. 54, 238.

out to us the influence of Christianity on human thought and its movements, out of which have come modern science and the industries to which science gives birth,' then the smile, if it came, could be, in my opinion, only the smile of ignorance or prejudice."

We may take another instance in illustration of our general position—the influence of Christianity on language. No words need be wasted in proving the intimate connection between language on the one side and human advancement or retrogression on the other. As man advances in civilization, as his world of thought enlarges, so language enlarges and grows richer. "As one habit of civilization after another is let go, the words which those habits demanded have dropped as well, first out of use and then out of memory, and thus after a while have been wholly lost."

Let us dwell for a few moments on this law under which language becomes more fruitful and more full. I do not know that it, and its bearing on the connection of Christianity with language, can be better stated than in the words of the present Archbishop of Dublin.

The "cause which more than any other creates the necessity for additions to the vocabulary of language, and evokes the words which shall supply this necessity when it is felt, is beyond a question this—namely, that in the appointments of highest Wisdom there are certain cardinal epochs in the world's history in which, far more than at other times, new moral and spiritual forces begin to work, and to stir society to its central depths. When it is thus with a people, they make claims upon their language which were never made upon it before. It is required to utter truths, to express ideas, which were strange to it in the time of its first moulding and shaping, and for which, therefore, terms sufficient will naturally not be found in it at once—these new thoughts and feelings being larger and deeper than any with which hitherto the speakers of that tongue had been familiar."

"The most illustrious example of this whereof I speak, is, of course, the coming in of Christianity, or, including the anterior dispensation, of revealed religion into the ancient heathen world, with the consequent necessity under which the great novel truths that were then proclaimed to mankind lay, to clothe themselves in the language of men, and first in the language of Greece and Rome; languages which in their previous form might have sufficed, and did suffice, for heathenism, sensuous and finite as it was, but not for the spiritual and infinite of the new dispensation."[28]

No man, indeed, but one who has carefully investigated the subject can have the smallest idea of the extent to which Christianity has permeated, vitalized, and enlarged the language of civilized nations; so that if you could eliminate from them its influence and work, you would not only greatly narrow their limits and abridge their fullness, but you would almost be compelled to learn them over again before you could use them intelligently. And then, besides, what a mass of the best and noblest literature must be utterly disfigured if not absolutely destroyed! This would be an invasion of barbarism in very truth.

Why, the very language in which unbelief voices its attacks on Christianity is language that largely owes its capacity to express the ideas that unbelievers seek to communicate, to the influence of Christianity itself.

It is, of course, easy to say that what is here asserted amounts to no more than the declaration that if Christianity had not existed it could

---

[28] Trench, *Study of Words*, p. 138–9.

not have been assailed; a declaration which would be simply a stupid truism. But the fallacy of such a reply is too obvious to need more than the merest mention. It is answered as soon as it is stated, and by its very statement.

There are, however higher things to be considered in civilization as vitalized by Christianity than science, industrial arts, language or letters. We have also to look at the moral training and advancement of civilized nations. Here is, after all, the crucial test. With this, we may well press upon men's thoughts the influence of Christianity in the various matters named, and in others like them. But without this, all those other things would amount to nothing, and would not be worth the trouble of considering. Let me then state this higher aspect of the influence of Christianity in the shortest and most comprehensive form: "The influence of Christianity on the moral education of nations is the great fact of modern times."

Now I know that I shall be met here with two objections, or it might, perhaps, be better said with two forms of the same objection. First it will be said, Talk as you will of the moral education of the nations by Christianity, any man can see that it has not wrought its purposed work. It speaks of peace and liberty and purity and mutual rights and duties, and we behold, on every side, war and oppression and impurity and manifold wrongs and evils. And then, secondly, we shall be told—we are told—that Christianity has not only failed in this wise and to this extent, but that it is itself the source of untold horrors that stain and darken the pages of the world's history. Such accusations as these burden, in our day, the very air.

Now underlying the answers to both these objections is the great fact, (conveniently overlooked just here, however loudly it may be asserted on other occasions) that Christianity, from the first, recognized the free agency of man as a moral being, and treated him as possessed of such free agency. On that basis, and on that basis only, it professed to do, it has done, its work.

Taking our stand, then, at this point, we may reply to the first objection: "Christianity has never acted, or professed to act, as a revolution, but only as a reform. It has never sought to produce unexpected, instant results, but it has gradually wrought the reform of minds and sentiments, and by the reform of morals and institutions the reform of the world. Such was its mission, such was the end it proposed, according to the declaration, "My Kingdom is not of this world;" that is to say, I do not act directly upon men in bodies as a civil law-giver, I reform the world by the reform of individuals."[29]

I suppose nothing is more frequently urged as proving the failure of Christianity in the moral training of the civilized nations than the wars and the armaments of those very nations. Now, admitting that "selfish ambition, rapacity, tyranny, and vanity" are largely the motives that bring about wars, and that "the condemnation of the one side is the justification of the other," that is to say, that the motives condemned on the one side justify resistance to them on the other; admitting that war may, sometimes, be the final and only method of obtaining justice when all others fail;[30] admitting that, for these reasons, armaments of nations are not to be sweepingly condemned, nor war indiscriminately branded as a crime; admitting all this, it is, assuredly, true that Christianity does propose to bring about peace on earth and good-will among, as well as to, men.

---

[29] Rossi, *Bibliothèque Universelle*, Dec. 1867.
[30] Mozley, *University Sermons*, Sermon V.

After all, it will be said, wars have not ceased in the world. No! but have they not become less frequent? Once they were unceasing in their continuous clang and clash; so unceasing that it was thought—and was—a marvellous thing when Christian influence caused the Truce of God [31] to be proclaimed, under which the din of arms was hushed from the evening of Wednesday to the morning of Monday in each week, and during Lent and Advent. Those periods of rest and safety to the people, giving them opportunity to turn to the arts of peace, were some gain surely. And there has been more gain since. Truces of God are the rule in our time rather than the exception, and the longer they continue the more old enmities are buried and forgotten. If some one had prophesied at Yorktown in September, 1781, that when the centennial of that victory, which secured their place as an imperial power to the United States, should be celebrated, the British flag would be honorably saluted, with the consent and even acclamation of the nation, what terms of contempt for his idiotic assertion would have been deemed too strong? Yet so it was. And what

---

[31] First proclaimed, probably, in 1032 or 1034.

brought it about? Not state-craft, not diplomacy, not human policy of any sort, but that drawing of heart to heart which obedience to the law of Christian sympathy had wrought. Time only strengthens such a bond as that!

Again, it will be said, the horrors and atrocities of war continue. Yes! but how much mitigated by Christian influences. When the Convention of Geneva recognized the neutrality of ambulances, and protected those who, marked with the cross of red, ministered to the wounded of either army, a great step was taken forward. Ministrations to the battle-stricken were indeed no new thing. Christian hearts had often before impelled men and women to undertake them. But recognition and protection of this sort were new things; and do they not, must they not, point on to a still better and brighter future?[32]

As to the second objection, that Christianity is itself the source of untold and horrible evils, it is even more futile than the first. It confounds, and that often for the basest purposes, what men, acting as free moral agents, have done under the name of Christianity, with the teach-

---

[32] Naville, *Le Christ*, p. 44.

ings and influence of Christianity itself. And this confusion the very men who make it would scorn and scout in other things. Who would hold law responsible for the chicanery of pettifoggers, or medicine for the pretences of quacks, or science for the charlatanry of empirics? In all these cases men easily distinguish between the character of the thing itself and the purposes and acts of those who attempt to use it as a cover for their own baseness and evil doing. Let the same obvious distinction be made here, let the same method of treatment be applied, and this objection vanishes at once. The reproach then falls on men and not on Christianity.

One word more before I leave this topic. It is surely a noteworthy fact that every scheme which contemplates the moral advancement of the race without accepting and employing the influences and laws of Christianity does, nevertheless, adopt as its necessary basis, those very moral rules which Christianity alone has given it. But for Christianity and its teachings, there would be nothing on which those who are now endeavoring to deny to Christianity and its institutions any share in the moral culture of the race, could take their stand. They owe to it the very position which but for it they could by no possibility assume.

The phenomenon which I have desired to present is now, I think, sufficiently before us to bring on the question which necessarily and at once grows out of it. The phenomenon is, first, that gathering up of what were the preparations of the past, when the Faith and the Church of Jesus Christ came into the world, and, next, that opening out of what was then the future, some of the manifold results of which we have been contemplating; a gathering up and an opening out which Christianity alone has wrought. The question is, how is this phenomenon to be accounted for, and what is its explanation?

Ridicule of human proneness to superstition, ridicule indeed of any kind, can neither destroy it nor explain its existence. That method was tried in the beginning much as it is tried to-day. "Some mocked" is the prophetic statement which follows the record of the sermon of St. Paul at Athens. In excavating the site of the palace of the Cæsars, at Rome, a room was found once occupied by the body-guard or the pages of the emperor. On its wall was roughly sketched the figure of a man bearing an ass's head and fastened to a cross; while underneath were the words "Alexamenes worships his God." No doubt the ribald soldier or flippant page who thus vented his contempt and scorn, thought he had given the *exitiabilis superstitio*—so Rome's great historian designates Christianity—its death-blow. No doubt applauding comrades gave praise to his achievment. To us it comes out of the dust and rubbish of centuries, so far as its author is concerned, simply as a saddening proof of human folly. But its misrepresentation of our Lord, the blasphemy of its caricature, its cheap and coarse attempt at wit have found their imitators in every age; they find them in our own. The uttered word and the written page have, indeed, taken the place of the rude sketch and legend, but both are outcomes of the same weak folly; and the same oblivion that came to one inevitably awaits the other.

The denial of the truths of history cannot destroy or explain the phenomenon. To deny, as the French writer quoted in my first lecture did, and as others have done since, that such a person as Jesus Christ ever existed, simply puts him who makes the denial outside the possibilities of discussion. No student of science would dream of attempting to discuss the solar system, as we term it, with one who began his part of the discussion by denying the existence of the central sun. In this case, indeed, it would be an undoubted scientific fact that would be denied, and in the other an attested fact of history. But he who makes the one denial outlaws himself from the domain of reasoning, as much as he who makes the other.

Do we gain anything in the way of explanation from the theory which first declares that in Jesus there abode the loftiest consciousness of God that humanity has ever known; which next asserts that in bringing the power of this consciousness to bear on man our Lord, when other means had failed, had recourse to falsehood, imposture, and the arts of a charlatan ; which, finally, in order to justify such crimes— for crimes they are—argues that mankind in order to be led must be deceived, and then concludes that, since no great work can be otherwise accomplished, such deceit is blameless? Now the ribald Roman soldier and his later imitators might very well adopt this theory. One who regarded Christianity as an evil thing might very well adopt it. But one who sees in Christianity a power for the good, the right, the true, can only protest, solemnly and earnestly, against such an outrage, not only upon God and upon our Lord, but upon the conscience of man and humanity itself. A pure stream could not proceed from so foul a source.

Do we make any advance towards a solution of the problem by saying that monotheism was natural to the Semitic race, especially to the Hebrews; that our Lord was a man of that race, of lofty character, reason, and conscience; that the reasonableness of his doctrine and the purity of his morals attracted a crowd of followers; that by these means his doctrine spread in the world; that, in time, a miraculous legend was formed, such as is often formed around good and great men; that, in a word, Christianity is the consummate flower of the "tree of religion," but is after all only the result of natural, aside from any supernatural, causes?

I have stated this theory, the latest, I believe, and the most attractive one, of the naturalistic school, almost in the words of an eloquent French writer, to whom I have already been indebted, and I will also give you the substance of his reply, with some of my own additions.

If monotheism was so natural to the Hebrews how was it that they were so perpetually lapsing into polytheism and idolatry; and that their strong tendencies in this direction were effectually checked only by the stern discipline of the Babylonian captivity? If the doctrine of Jesus of Nazareth *satisfies* in many things the reason, does it not also *confound* the reason by the mysteries for which it demands belief? If it *consoles* the heart on the one hand, does it not also *lacerate* it on the other, in demanding the sacrifice of its deepest affections in the cause of duty and of God? If it *calms* the conscience by its promises of pardon, does it not also *disturb* it by the strictness of its requirements? So far, then, as we contemplate its attractions for individual's souls we find over against every one of them a balancing, if not an overbalancing, obstacle.

And if we look on things external we really see scarce anything but obstacles, obstacles that are, apparently, insurmountable; the hatred of the Jew, the scorn of the Greek, the "superb contempt" of the Roman; on every side persecution, prisons, torture, death; nothing to favor the advancement of the "sect everywhere spoken against," everything to oppose it. And yet we behold it ever spreading, ever overcoming difficulties, ever gathering new adherents, till Tertullian could say,[33] "We are of yesterday, and yet we have filled your cities, islands, castles, towns, your places of assembly, your very camps, your tribes, your decuriæ, the palace, the senate, the forum; we have left you only your temples;" till the last confessedly heathen emperor, dying on the plains of Persia, was compelled to cry with his latest breath, as he flung a handful of his own blood up towards heaven, "Galilean, Thou hast conquered!"[34]

Whether, then, we consider the internal or the external difficulties of the naturalistic solution of our problem, it breaks down by its own weight. Driven thus from one explanation to another, and finding none to meet the conditions of the phenomenon we have in mind, and to explain them, we are also driven—if I may so say—to the account which Christianity gives of itself, namely, that it is God's plan for the regeneration of the race. This explains, adequately and fully, how it lives by death, conquers by what seems to men's eyes failures, grows by repression, is strong in its weakness,

---

[33] *Apolog.* c. xxxvii.
[34] Theodoret, *Eccl. Hist.* Lib. III. c. xxv. One cannot but think that Julian's words meant more than merely a reference to his own death.

rich in its poverty, glorious in its humiliation; because it is the power of God and the wisdom of God.

Am I told that if one accepts this explanation he also accepts the idea of a miraculous interposition of God in the affairs of men, and that this involves too severe a strain on faith? Then I reply, that any other explanation involves a vastly greater strain, and compels me to accept a vastly greater miracle; for, you may rely upon it, incredulity is the most credulous of all things.

If Christianity has won its way and done its work because it is a puerile superstition and a fair butt for ribald wit; or because its reputed Founder never lived on earth; or because with lofty purposes and aims He still condescended to arts of deceit and charlatancy, thereby outraging both God and man; or because against every attraction which it presented a fully balancing obstacle reared itself, against every outward favoring circumstance there stood an overbalancing counter-circumstance that seemed to be an insurmountable hindrance; if I am to seek in these things the explanation of the spread and the work of Christianity among men, then, indeed, I am presented with a miracle, or rather a mass of miracles, that well may stagger me. While I have been asserting the impossibility of any miracle, I have been creating a thousand for myself. While I have been making boast of my philosophical incredulity, I have fallen into the pit of a most unphilosophical credulity. And my only escape from it is to accept the account which Christianity gives of itself, its origin, its Founder, its purposes and its powers. In that light, and in that light only, shall we see light, the light in which there is no darkness at all.

As I draw toward the end of the line of thought along which we have been moving, I am reminded that I have not brought out those loftiest truths with which we find ourselves in contact, nor led you to that higher level on which we stand, when we consider the living power of the truth as it is in Jesus on human character in its individual personality ; in a word, the life of God in the soul of man. This has not been because I underestimate the surpassing value and reality of this great attestation of the Faith. God forbid ! But, only because my purpose was to show, if I might, that looking solely at what the Faith and the Church of Jesus Christ had accomplished for the race in the outworkings of its ordinary historical development, the truest explanation—indeed, the only one that met all the conditions of the phenomenon to be explained—was found in their own account of their original power as being from God, and not of man.

But that the higher and at the same time the deeper thought may not be quite omitted, let us place ourselves once more at the point towards which, as we have seen, all previous history converges, from which all after historic life and movement diverge. Doing this, we find ourselves standing, as the Apostles once stood, in "the coasts of Cæsarea Philippi" and by the side of Jesus. We know, as we stand there, what they did not—the story of the future. We hear the question, "Whom do men say that I, the Son of man, am?" We hear the Apostles' answer as to the men of that day—but we hear more. From the future, of which they knew nothing, we hear a confused sound of many voices in reply. Some say a deceiver; others, the ideal man; still others, one who was the joint production of climate, race, and surrounding conditions and circumstances; others still, one in whom the divine has temporarily rested in the progress of its eternally recurring incarnations. Amid all the perplexity and confusion another question reaches us, "Whom say ye that I am?" And as we look back through preceding and on through coming ages, what answer can we give but the one that Peter gave, "Thou art the Christ, the Son of the living God"?

Surely we cannot rest there. Surely we must ask, you and I, What do these answers promise *me?* To what do they bring me? What is built upon them, what comes out from them, for me and my own necessities? Whatever it is and whatever it means, no reply can be anything to me, unless it is individually my own, and unless it means something for me as an individual. What is to be said, then, of these several replies?

If I conclude that Jesus was a deceiver, nothing is offered me. If I say that He was an, or even the, ideal man, I am brought in contact with an example—possibly with a school of morals—but with nothing more. If I regard Him as one developed by manifold natural conditions, or one in whom the divine temporarily rested, then I find "an ideal Christianity; a religion free, individual, without dogma or bond of union, without theology or church; a religion eclectic and sentimental, which each man builds up for himself according to his own individual notion of God, admitting under that name, so vague and confused, all great men and moralists; so building for the future a Jerusalem which De Sacy thus describes: 'a Jerusalem with a hundred gates, on which is written beside the name of Moses that of Mohammed, beside the name of Jesus that of Buddha, beside the names of St. Peter and St. Paul those of Rousseau and Voltaire; a Jerusalem which bears a marvellous likeness to the tower of Babel, save that the old Babel *ended* with a confusion of tongues, and this new one *begins* with a confusion of ideas.'" [35]

On the other hand, if Jesus be the Christ, the Son of the living God, then there is offered me the sacrifice of the cross, the power of the Resurrection, the life of the Spirit; a way, a truth, a life, which meet my deepest needs and satisfy my highest longings. Then I find that vision of peace, that city of God over against the city of the world, that New Jerusalem which does not spring up from the earth to go back into the earth again, but which " cometh

---

[35] Caro, *L'idée de Dieu et les Nouveaux Critiques*, p. 130.

down from heaven," and takes up and uses for man on earth what man has failed to use for himself; and so uses what it thus takes up as to build, not merely for the race as a mass but for each single soul, not for time alone but also for eternity, "a city that hath foundations." This gathers up the past, this opens out the future, for every living man.

> Built on the living Corner Stone
>   The city of our God doth rise,
> Bright vision of celestial peace,
>   Whose jewelled turrets pierce the skies;
> While in deep ranks on every side
>   Angels surround the Saviour's Bride!
> How blest the mystic bond that binds
>   Thee, dowered with glories all divine,
> Shining in marriage gifts of grace,
>   Queen Mother of a princely line,
> To Christ thy Lord in spousal given,
>   Gleaming Jerusalem of heaven!

1881.

FOUNDER'S DAY

AT

Kenyon College.

FOUNDER'S DAY.

ORDER OF SERVICE

FOR

ALL SAINTS' DAY.

November 1st, 1881.

OFFICIATING PERSONS.

THE TE DEUM.

ANTE-COMMUNION, . . . { Right Reverend George Wm. Peterkin, D.D., of West Virginia.

THE EPISTLE, ... { Rev. W. C. French, D.D., Secretary of Convention.

THE GOSPEL, ... { Rev. W. B. Bodine, D.D., President of the College.

CREED, ... { Rev. Fleming James, D.D., Pastor.

FOUNDER'S MEMORIAL, . . { Right Reverend Gregory Thurston Bedell, D.D., of Ohio.

DOXOLOGY.

PRAYER FOR INSTITUTIONS.

HYMN 183.

THE LECTURE, ... { Right Reverend John Williams, D.D., of Connecticut.

HYMN 176.

OFFERTORY FOR FOUNDER'S SCHOLARSHIP.

PRAYER FOR CHURCH MILITANT.

MATRICULATION OF THE THEOLOGICAL SEMINARY.

MATRICULATION OF KENYON COLLEGE.

THE HOLY COMMUNION, administered by the Bishops present.

BENEDICTION, by the Right Reverend the Bishop of Connecticut.

FOUNDER'S DAY
AT KENYON COLLEGE, 1881.

WE REMEMBER BEFORE GOD this day the Founders of these Institutions: PHILANDER CHASE, the first Bishop of Ohio, *clarum et venerabile nomen*, whose foresight, zeal, unwearied patience, and indomitable energy, devised these foundations, and established them, temporarily at Worthington, but permanently at Gambier. He was the founder of the Theological Seminary, Kenyon College, and of the Grammar School;—CHARLES PETTIT MCILVAINE, the second Bishop of Ohio, rightly known as the second Founder of these Institutions, whose decision of character, and self-devoted labors, saved them at two distinct crises of difficulty; he builded Bexley Hall for the use of the Theological Seminary, Ascension Hall for the use of Kenyon College, Milnor Hall for the use of the Grammar School, and he completed Rosse Chapel on the foundations laid by Bishop Chase.

We remember before God this day pious and generous persons, contributors, whose gifts enabled the Bishops of Ohio to lay those foundations, and who are therefore to be named among the Founders. We make mention only of those who have departed to be with Christ, and now rest in Paradise.

Among the many, we name only a few whose gifts are noticeable because of the influence of their character and position:

HENRY CLAY, whose introduction of Bishop Chase to the ADMIRAL LORD GAMBIER, of England, initiated the movement in 1823; the ARCHBISHOP of Canterbury; the LORD BISHOPS of London, Durham, St. Davids, Chester, Lichfield; the DEANS of Canterbury and Salisbury; LORDS Kenyon, Gambier, Bexley, Sir Thomas Acland; Reverend Edward Bickersteth, Henry Hoare, Marriott, Pratt, WILLIAM WILBERFORCE, Thomas Wiggin, Thomas Bates; the Dowager COUNTESS OF ROSSE, who aided liberally the Chapel which afterwards bore her name; HANNAH MORE, who also bequeathed a Scholarship which bears her name; and five hundred and thirty others whose names are recorded in the memorial prepared by the Rev. Dr. Bronson at the order of the Trustees.

We remember before God the liberality of WILLIAM HOGG, from whom this domain was purchased under the advice of Henry B. Curtis and Daniel S. Norton, with the consent of Henry Clay; the grantor contributing one fourth of its market value.

In 1838, JOHN QUINCY ADAMS, the President of the

United States; Mrs. Sigourney; Arthur Tappan, who originated the Milnor Professorship; St. George's Church, New York, which established a Scholarship; Rev. Drs. Milnor, Tyng, Bedell, Sparrow, Keith, Rev. I. Morse, Dudley Chase, Albert Barnes, John Trimble, William Jay, Abbott and Amos Lawrence, Peter Stuyvesant, Richard Varick, and nine hundred and ninety others whose names are recorded.

These were the first Founders of these Institutions.

Among those who aided Bishop McIlvaine we mention before God to-day,—in 1832, BISHOP WHITE, Rev. Manton Eastburn and the Ascension Church, the Rev. Dr. Cutler and St. Ann's Church, Brooklyn, the Rev. Drs. Muhlenberg, and Wing, Peter A. Jay, James Lennox, Robert Minturn, Henry Codman, Robert Carter, Matthew Clarkson, Charles Hoyt, J. N. Whiting, and four hundred and sixty others whose names are recorded.

And in 1835, in England, Daniel Wilson, Bishop of Calcutta; the Bishops of London, Winchester, Salisbury, and Lichfield; the DUCHESS OF KENT, the Duchess of Gloucester, the Princess Augusta, the Duchess of Beaufort, the Earl of Carnarvon, Rev. Thomas Hartwell Horne, Charles Brydges, John Fox, Jerram, Jowett, Baptist Noel, Dr. Plumtre, Charles Simeon, Henry Thornton, Sir Thomas Baring, Henry Roberts, architect, who gave the plan and working model for

Bexley Hall; with four hundred and eighty-three others whose names are recorded.

These are the second Founders of these Institutions.

We mention before God to-day the gifts of Bishop Gadsden, Bishop Johns, Colonel Pendleton, John Kilgour, the Kinneys, Dr. Doddridge, Charles D. Betts, who founded a fund for the purchase of theological books; Rev. C. C. Pinkney, who contributed for fitting up a Laboratory; J. D. Wolfe, who contributed to found the Lorillard and Wolfe Professorships; John Johns, M.D., of Baltimore, who left a valuable legacy to the Institutions; Stewart Brown, William H. Aspinwall, and others who contributed to the building of Ascension Hall; Thomas H. Powers, Lewis S. Ashurst, John Bohlen and sister, and others who founded a Professorship in memory of the late Dr. Bedell of Philadelphia; W. W. Corcoran, President Andrews, Rev. Alfred Blake, and nine hundred and forty-four others who are also to be counted among the founders of these Institutions.

And last, the Philanthropist, the intimate friend of Bishop McIlvaine, who in token of that friendship founded a Professorship, that now bears his name, bears the name of GEORGE PEABODY.

The donors to these Institutions who are still living (many of whom have gathered on this day) unite with us in praising God for the privilege of building upon foundations which were thus so strongly laid.

Among them we mention with gratitude,—of England, WILLIAM E. GLADSTONE, Member of Parliament (at present Prime Minister), Rev. Canon Carus, and J. Pye Smith;—of the United States, Rev. Drs. Dyer and Burr, Professor Francis Wharton, A. H. Moss, M. M. Granger, John Gardiner, Mrs. Spencer, Rev. Archibald M. Morrison, who founded the Griswold Professorship; Peter Neff, Jr., who gave the Telescope, and Transit Instrument; Mrs. Lewis, who partly founded a Professorship; the Rev. Drs. Muenscher, Bronson, and Brooke; Rev. Messrs. Lounsbury and E. A. Strong, whose efforts brought many valuable contributions to these Institutions; and several hundred others whose names are recorded.

The third Bishop of Ohio, with the aid of William H. and John Aspinwall, James M. Brown, Samuel D. Babcock, William B. Astor, and other members of the Ascension Church of New York, builded the Church of the Holy Spirit for the use of all the Institutions; through him Mrs. Bowler founded the Professorship which bears her husband's name, R. B. Bowler, who gave a philosophical apparatus, and who with Larz Anderson, Henry Probasco, William Proctor, and others, founded the McIlvaine Professorship; Jay Cooke founded the Professorship which bears his father's name; Frank E. Richmond founded the Hoffman Library Fund; Stewart Brown builded the Tower of the Church, to bear the name of his son, Abbott Brown. By the same Bishop and his wife the Organ was placed in the Church as a memorial of the second Bishop of the Diocese, and the Episcopal chair as a memorial of the great Founder; R. S. French with the assistance of friends provided the full Chime of nine Bells and the Clock, and by the aid of citizens of Gambier and Mount Vernon placed them in the Church-tower with power to ring the Canterbury Chimes; members of the Church in Philadelphia completed the endowment of the Bedell Professorship, among them chiefly William Welsh, John Bohlen and his sister, and Thomas H. Powers, who also left a Fund in the hands of the Vestry of Christ Church, Germantown, for a perpetual supply of specified books for students in Bexley Hall; and Robert S. Ives and his wife, who stated that, desiring not to trammel the Trustees, they placed their fund in the Treasury without conditions.

In 1875 the Trustees determined to found a "Trustees' Professorship," which is partially completed.

All these and seventy others are also to be counted among the Founders.

We mention with gratitude the successful efforts of the present President of Kenyon College to complete the endowments, and the gifts which have resulted therefrom; namely, from R. B. HAYES, PRESIDENT OF THE UNITED STATES, Peter Hadyn, Dr. I. T. Hobbs, Rev. William Horton, Thomas McCulloch, Samuel L. Mather, William J. Boardman, A. C. Armstrong, H. P. Baldwin; from John W. Andrews a donation in lands for the founding of Scholarships in memory of his son; from Mrs. Alfred Blake donations for the purpose of founding a Scholarship to bear her husband's name; from Columbus Delano the Hall which bears his name; from Mrs. Ezra Bliss a Gymnasium which is being built; and from Henry B. Curtis, Scholarships which from generation to generation will foster sound learning. These also with thirty others, the latest givers to our Institutions, are to be counted among the Founders.

The congregation rising.

For all these generous gifts of the living, and for the memory of the dead who were the FOUNDERS of these Institutions, we give hearty thanks to God this day; ascribing the praise of their benefactions to His almighty grace, and the glory to His most holy Name, who is the God of our fathers and our God, the Father, the Son, and the Holy Ghost, ONE ADORABLE TRINITY for ever and ever. Amen.

www.ingramcontent.com/pod-product-compliance
Lightning Source LLC
Chambersburg PA
CBHW020226090426
42735CB00010B/1606